A Guide for Using

Our Only May Amelia

in the Classroom

Based on the novel written by Jennifer L. Holm

*This guide written by **Allison Morse-Griswold***

Teacher Created Materials, Inc.
6421 Industry Way
Westminster, CA 92683
www.teachercreated.com
©2004 Teacher Created Materials
Made in U.S.A.
ISBN 0-7439-3161-0

Edited by
Melissa Hart, M.F.A.

Illustrated by
Alexandra Artigas

Cover Art by
Kevin Barnes

Table of Contents

Introduction

A good book can touch our lives like a good friend. Within its pages are words and characters that can inspire us to achieve our highest ideals. We can turn to it for companionship, recreation, comfort, and guidance. It can also give us a cherished story to hold in our hearts forever.

Great care has been taken in literature units to select books that are sure to become good friends!

Teachers who use this literature unit will find the following features to supplement their own valuable ideas:

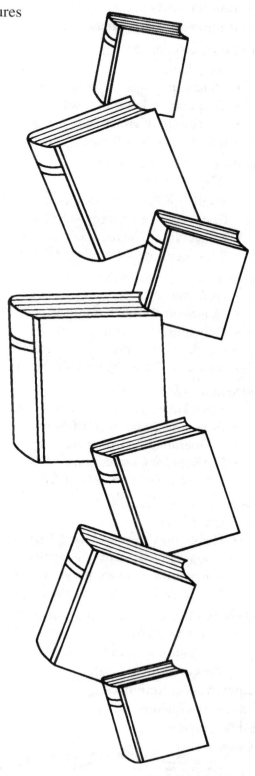

- Sample Lesson Plans

- Pre-reading Activities

- Biographical Sketch and Picture of Author

- Book Summary

- Vocabulary Lists and Suggested Vocabulary Ideas

- Chapters grouped for study with each section including:
    —quizzes

    —hands-on projects

    —cooperative learning activities

    —cross-curricular connections

    —extensions into the reader's own life

- Post-reading Activities

- Book Project Ideas

- Research Ideas

- Culminating Activities

- Three Different Options for Unit Tests

- Bibliography

- Answer Key

We are confident that this unit will be a valuable addition to your planning, and we hope that as you use our ideas, your students will increase their circle of literary "friends."

Sample Lesson Plans

Each of the lessons suggested below takes one or more days to complete.

Lesson 1
- Introduce and have students complete some or all of the pre-reading activities found on (page 5).
- Read "About the Author" with your students. (page 6)
- Read the book summary with students. (page 7)
- Introduce the vocabulary list for Section 1. (page 8)

Lesson 2
- Read chapters 1 and 2. As you read, place the vocabulary words in the context of the story and discuss their meanings.
- Complete a vocabulary activity. (page 9)
- Make Laksloda (salmon casserole). (page 11)
- Identify and discuss characters. (page 12)
- Discuss the book in terms of science. (page 13)
- Begin "Readers' Response Journals." (page 14)
- Administer the Section 1 quiz. (page 10)
- Introduce the vocabulary for Section 2. (page 8)

Lesson 3
- Read Chapters 3 through 5. Place the vocabulary words in context and discuss their meanings.
- Complete a vocabulary activity. (page 9)
- Learn about rowing on the river. (page 16)
- Chart May's roots in a family tree. (page 17)
- Discuss the book in terms of geography. (page 18)
- Show appreciation through a letter. (page 19)
- Administer the Section 2 quiz. (page 15)
- Introduce the vocabulary for Section 3. (page 8)

Lesson 4
- Read Chapters 6 through 8. Place the vocabulary words in context and discuss their meanings.
- Complete a vocabulary activity. (page 9)
- Do math to calculate the speed of logs travelling down the river. (page 21)

- Act out the personalities of characters. (page 22)
- Compute gender probabilities. (page 23)
- Create words out of your name. (page 24)
- Administer the Section 3 quiz. (page 20)
- Introduce the vocabulary for Section 4. (page 8)

Lesson 5
- Read Chapters 9 and 10. Place the vocabulary words in context and discuss their meanings.
- Complete a vocabulary activity. (page 9)
- Make a scrapbook page. (page 26)
- Re-enact a scene from the book using puppets. (page 27)
- Learn about how logging endangers animals. (page 28)
- Share baby books with classmates. (page 29)
- Administer the Section 4 quiz. (page 25)
- Introduce the vocabulary for Section 5. (page 8)

Lesson 6
- Read Chapters 11 through 13. Place the vocabulary words in context and discuss their meanings.
- Complete a vocabulary activity. (page 9)
- Learn to use chopsticks. (page 31)
- Share a journal entry. (page 32)
- Translate words from English to Finnish to Chinese. (page 33)
- Compare yourself to May Amelia. (page 34)
- Administer the Section 5 quiz. (page 30)

Lesson 7
- Discuss questions students may have about story. (page 35)
- Assign book report and research projects. (pages 36–37)
- Display and discuss newspaper culminating activity. (pages 38–39)
- Plan and enjoy a Finnish-themed party. (pages 40–42)
- Administer unit test 1, 2, or 3. (pages 43–45)
- Discuss the test answers and responses.
- Provide a bibliography of related reading for the students. (page 46)

Before the Book

Before you begin reading *Our Only May Amelia*, it will benefit students to understand the time period and cultural framework in which the book is set. Pre-reading activities will help students to focus on the story. Here are some ideas that may work well in your classroom.

1. Predict what the story might be about by hearing the title.

2. Predict what the story might be about by looking at the cover illustration.

3. Discuss the genre of historical fiction.

4. Individually or in small groups, write brief, fictionalized accounts of significant events in your country's history.

5. Discuss what life was like in 1899 in Washington as a Finnish settler.

6. Answer the questions below:

   Are you interested in:

   • stories that take place long ago?

   • stories about playing pranks on siblings?

   • stories about children who are constantly getting into mischief?

   Would you ever:

   • toss your brother into a pigpen full of mud?

   • be able to take care of a newborn baby?

   • be able to cope with the loss of a family member?

   • be able to live with people other than your parents for a few months?

7. In groups, pairs, or individually, write or discuss the meaning of the word *only*. Have you ever been the "only" something or someone? What do you think May Amelia is the "only" one of?

About the Author

Jennifer Holm grew up in Audubon, Pennsylvania, with four brothers. She has fond memories of climbing trees, building forts, and fishing with them. Jennifer studied International Studies at Dickinson College in Carlisle, Pennsylvania. She first became interested in writing when she took a creative writing class during her senior year.

Jennifer's inspiration for *Our Only May Amelia* came from a unique Christmas gift she received. One Christmas, her family passed down to her a cherished diary, which was written by her great-aunt when she was between the ages of 12 and 18. Jennifer's great-aunt, Alice Amelia Holm, was a Finnish-American girl born on the Nasel River in Washington State during the nineteenth century. Although Alice only wrote small entries in her diary, they gave Jennifer ideas for the speech and anecdotes of her main character. The diary mentioned experiences similar to Jennifer's—experiences which would become those of May Amelia. Some of these experiences are playing tricks on her brothers, going fishing, and travelling on the Nasel to visit cousins. Those incidents and some of the landmarks used in the novel were taken right from the diary. Jennifer combined truths from her own life with Alice's story to develop May Amelia's childhood.

Jennifer Holm received the Newbery Honor Award from the American Library Association in 2000 for *Our Only May Amelia*. She often writes books which are narrated by female main characters, though she also hoped to appeal to a male audience with the depiction of May's brothers. In *Our Only May Amelia*, she wanted to show that families can be complicated, and that different types of relationships exist between different family members.

Besides creating memorable female heroines, Holm is interested in writing about history and real events. She continues to work on new releases of the Boston Jane series. The two books already published in this series are *Boston Jane: An Adventure*, and *Boston Jane: Wilderness Days*. This series is about a young woman who leaves Philadelphia to meet her fiancé in the wilderness of Washington. The books are filled with history, adventure, and romance. Her latest book is called *The Creek*. This is her first contemporary, suspense novel. In *The Creek*, a young teen grows up in the suburbs of Philadelphia, facing the challenge of being stuck between childhood and adulthood.

Our Only May Amelia

by Jennifer L. Holm

(HarperCollins Publishers, 1999)

May Amelia is the only daughter in a family of eight children. In fact, May is the only girl in the entire Nasel settlement in Washington. May faces daily challenges because she wants to be able to do everything that her brothers can do. She is tired of being treated like a girl who can only have limited adventures.

Her father continually reminds her that she can't do things because she is a girl. But being female doesn't stop May Amelia in her desire to find adventure. The fact that she is often told to act like a "proper young lady" only drives her to more mischief. She plays pranks on her brothers, and participates in the boys' pranks on other people, too. She is definitely not the neat and elegant female her father would like her to be.

As May continues to stir up mischief, her mother gives birth to a baby girl. May is thrilled by this. She is even allowed to select the baby's name. May's mother becomes ill after the baby is born, and May takes over the responsibilities for the baby. May is devastated when baby Amy dies for no apparent reason only a short time after her birth. She is back to being the only girl on the Nasel River.

May Amelia goes to stay with her aunt in Astoria because she cannot bear to be reminded of Amy's memory in the house. At her aunt's house, she meets the first girlfriend of her life. Her girlfriend, Emma, is a proper lady. The two girls balance each other out in their frolics, one "tomboy" and one a prim and proper "lace-and-hankies girl." May learns that being a girl isn't so horrible.

May returns home after she has mourned Amy's death, having matured and become wiser. She realizes that she is loved and needed in her household. She doesn't mind the responsibilities that are put upon her as much as she did before she went to Astoria. She realizes that being the "only" May Amelia isn't so bad after all.

Vocabulary Lists

The vocabulary lists on this page correspond to each sectional grouping of chapters, as outlined in the Table of Contents (page 2). Vocabulary activity ideas can be found on page 9 of this book.

Section 1

abiding	gill-netter	roughriders
accursed	gunnysack	shanghai
ambush	harlots	shivaree
bateau	hinder	snags
cunning	homestead	swindlers
dungarees	ornery	unison
dysentery	predicament	venison
exasperated	reluctantly	

Section 2

abide	infuriate	scandalous
belligerently	mahogany	slovenly
clabbered	mucking	smirking
defy	mutton	swaddled
fancies	ominously	threadbare
grouses	ornery	urchin
hellion	poultice	veranda
homestead		

Section 3

banished	gallivanting	scoundrel
clomping	gurgles	skeptically
clutches	hovering	superstition
conspiring	irresponsible	suspended
curtly	jargon	teat
dredging	parlour	tolerate
embroidery	retching	traipsing

Section 4

camphor	gnarled	provisions
exaggeration	grimly	slur
fricasseed	jostling	smugglers
floes	moored	vagabonds
glowering	obliged	

Section 5

acquaintance	devours	lye
beseechingly	eloped	notions
calico	hex	petticoats
cannery	hoists	rapscallions
craggy	lunatic	wryly

8

Vocabulary Activity Ideas

You can help students to reinforce, learn, and retain the vocabulary in *Our Only May Amelia* with these vocabulary activities:

- Give vocabulary pre-tests. Eliminate the words students already know. Create individualized vocabulary lists and quizzes.

- Challenge students to use as many of the vocabulary terms as they can in one logical sentence.

- Take original sentences from the book, which include targeted vocabulary words. Ask students to rewrite the sentences by inserting synonyms in place of the vocabulary words. Encourage students to use a thesaurus, and welcome variation and creativity.

- Create Crossword Puzzles or Wordsearch Puzzles, using graph paper, or website templates on the computer.

- Play Vocabulary Charades. In this game, vocabulary words are acted out, using the same techniques found in a traditional game of charades.

- Keep a Vocabulary Diary. Students write all the vocabulary words down in a small notebook. They must get a parent or teacher to initial the word every time they use it throughout the course of a week.

- Create an Illustrated Dictionary by drawing illustrations for each vocabulary word.

- Ask your students to create paragraphs which use vocabulary words to present history lessons relating to the time period mentioned in the story.

- Play Twenty Clues with the class. In this game, one student selects a vocabulary word and gives clues about the word, one by one, until someone in the class can guess the word.

- Play Guess the Definition. One student writes down the correct definition of the vocabulary word. The others write down false definitions, close enough to the original definition that their classmates might be fooled. Read all definitions, and then challenge students to guess the correct one. The students whose definitions mislead their classmates get a point for each student fooled.

- Write the words with glue on stiff paper, and then cover the glue with glitter or sand. Alternatively, students may write the words on toast with a squeeze bottle full of jam, creating an edible lesson!

Add your own ideas to this list. Practicing selected words through fun activities increases student interest in, and retention of, vocabulary words.

Answer the following questions from ch

1. Who is May Amelia Jackson? _____ _____

_____

2. Why is May Amelia considered "only"? _____

_____

3. Why does May Amelia prefer Wilbert over all her brothers? _____

_____

4. Why does May Amelia refer to herself as "a no-good girl"? _____

_____

5. Why does Wilbert believe that Baby Island is cursed? _____

_____

6. How does May Amelia get the opportunity to go to Astoria for the first time?

_____

_____

7. Describe one of the stops May Amelia and her brothers make along the way to Astoria.

_____

_____

8. What trick do the twins play on May at the end of the delicious dinner?

_____

_____

9. Name two ways that the Nasel settlement is different from Astoria.

_____

_____

10. Explain the differences between May Amelia's mother and her Aunt Alice.

_____

_____

Making Laksloda
Salmon Casserole

Salmon is an important part of the Finnish-American diet. Aunt Alice serves hers with a cream sauce and says it is "English food." This recipe is for the traditional Finnish dish called Laksloda, or salmon casserole. It is similar to what May and her brothers eat at their aunt's house. Prepare this recipe as a class, or make it at your house. Before serving, check with the school nurse for students' food allergies. Serve small portions, as this isn't meant to be a meal—just a taste-test.

Ingredients:

- 3 cups (709.8 ml) whole milk
- 5–6 peeled and washed potatoes
- ½ tsp. (2.45 ml) salt
- ½ tsp. (2.45 ml) pepper

- ½ lb. (227 grams) fresh, skinless salmon
- ½ stick butter
- 4 Tbsp. (59.2 ml) flour
- 1 onion (optional)

Materials:

- medium-sized casserole dish with cover
- cutting board

- sharp knife (do not allow students to handle)

Directions:

Preheat oven to 350° F (165° C). Slice the potatoes and onions (if desired) into slices about ½" (.6 cm) thick. Cut salmon into chunks about 1" (2.4 cm) in size. Use 1 Tbsp. (14.8 ml) of butter to grease the casserole dish. Put in enough potatoes and onion slices to fill up half of the casserole dish. Add salmon chunks on top of potato and onion slices. Sprinkle the salmon layer with flour. Cover the floured salmon with the remainder of the potato and onion slices. Pour milk over the top of potatoes and onions until it covers the potatoes. Do not put too much milk in, or else it will boil over the top. Add the remainder of the butter, cut into small chunks. Finally, add salt and pepper. Cover dish and bake at 350° F (165 ° C) for an hour and 15 minutes, or until golden brown.

Larger Than Life

May Amelia certainly has a large family! She has so many brothers that it is hard to keep track of who is who. This activity will help you establish who the characters are and ensure that you do not get the brothers confused.

Using large pieces of construction paper, sketch each character in the book. You may draw just their heads, or draw their whole bodies. Cut out the characters. Another option is to use construction paper without cutting it out into characters; just write the names of the characters on the top. Decide as a class which would be the better method.

1. Break into small groups. Each group begins with a different character cut-out. For five minutes, brainstorm on the physical and personality traits of your character.

2. As you brainstorm the characteristics, write them down on the construction paper cut-out.

3. At the end of five minutes, it is time to rotate. You can rotate groups by moving the students around or by rotating the character posters themselves around. The timer is set again and the brainstorming of personality and physical traits resumes. After reading what the first group has already written, the second group now adds to the list of character traits on the same poster.

4. This procedure should continue until all groups of students have had a chance to add to all character posters. It gets more and more challenging as the rounds go on, because the lists of character traits have grown steadily. Groups will find themselves growing increasingly more creative with their adjectives.

Students may continue to add to the character charts as they read on in the story.

"Red at Night, Seaman's Delight."

Ivan says, "Red at night, seaman's delight; bloody in the morning, sailor takes warning." He means that if the sky is red in the morning, a storm is on its way.

American Indians know that most natural events, such as the appearance of certain insects and the bloom of wildflowers, occur in the same order, year after year. They use this knowledge to decide when to plant certain crops. In recent times, the use of environmental and climate clues has become a branch of science called *phenology*. Ivan's quote is based on the natural observations he uses to govern life's activities.

Here are several other phenological sayings:

- When the sun goes to bed red, 'twill rain tomorrow, it's said.
- When wasps build their nests in exposed areas, expect a dry season.
- When elm leaves are the size of a penny, plant green beans.
- When peach and plum trees bloom, plant hardy crops like asparagus, rhubarb, and strawberries.

1. Brainstorm as a class to come up with more phenological sayings. Continue the brainstorming as a homework assignment.

2. After the class has brainstormed and polled family members, conduct a class discussion of the phenological sayings. Use the following questions to guide your discussion.

   a. Are there some sayings that are common? _____

   _____

   b. Are there some that are quite unusual? _____

   _____

   c. Are there certain sayings that are used in some cultures, but not in others?_____

   _____

   d. Are there variations in sayings between the different generations? _____

   _____

   e. What other professions (aside from farmers) could benefit from phenology?_____

   _____

   f. How could knowing some of these quotes be useful to you in your life?_____

   _____

   g. How might phenology affect the way nurseries conduct business? _____

   _____

Readers' Response Journals

Keeping a journal is important while reading this novel. Most of the ideas and characters for *Our Only May Amelia* were created based on the journal entries in an actual diary. Journal writing while reading draws students into literature on a personal level. It triggers readers' imagination, makes them think, and connects them to characters by bringing out their own feelings. Here are a few ways you can help your students think on an interpersonal level while using Readers' Response Journals. Continue to use these journal ideas throughout the entire novel.

- Tell students that the purpose of a journal is to record their thoughts, ideas, observations, and questions as they read *Our Only May Amelia*.

- Provide students with, or have them suggest, topics from the story that may inspire writing. Here are two examples from the chapters in Section 1.

  —May Amelia is the "only" girl in her family. She is also the only young girl in the entire settlement in which she lives. How does she feel about being the only girl? Write about a situation in which you have been the "only" someone or something. Describe your feelings at the time. Would you say the experience was more positive or negative?

  —When May first arrives at Aunt Alice's, she mentally makes a comparison between her aunt and her mother, who are sisters. Take another look at the contrast she draws on page 10. What different paths have the women's lives taken that would contribute to these differences? Why do you think the two sisters are so different? Compare and contrast your relationship with one of your own siblings. In what ways are you similar to and/or different from this sibling?

- After reading each chapter, students can write one or more new things they have learned about May Amelia.

- Read part of a chapter and stop reading at a "cliff-hanger." Ask students to write about what they think will happen next.

- Ask students to re-write part of the chapter with a different twist on the ending. For example, in Chapter 6, what might have happened if May had gone to the dance with her brothers?

- Students might choose to write their journal responses from a particular character's perspective.

Answer the following questions from chapters 3 through 5.

1. Why does everyone continually tell May Amelia that she is a miracle? _____

   _____

   _____

2. What do Isaiah and May witness at Baby Island?_____

   _____

   _____

3. Who comes to May Amelia's aid when she is injured on Baby Island?_____

   _____

   _____

4. What is the secret that Matti confides to May Amelia? _____

   _____

   _____

5. Describe the practical joke May plays on Kaarlo. _____

   _____

   _____

6. How is it that Kaarlo comes to be a member of the family? _____

   _____

   _____

7. How does the family feel when Kaarlo leaves? _____

   _____

   _____

8. What are two things that Grandmother Patience tries to change in the household?

   _____

   _____

   _____

9. What does Wilbert do when he realizes that May has been physically injured by their
   grandmother? _____

   _____

   _____

10. Describe the events that lead up to Grandmother Patience breaking May's doll.

   _____

   _____

   _____

Rollin' on the River

The Nasel River is vital to the Jackson family's transportation. They rely on the river for travel to school, relatives' houses, and the funeral grounds. For the Jacksons, life would not be possible without rowboats. One of May's wishes is that Pappa will allow her to go in a boat all by herself, without her brothers.

Teacher note: Students will create a boat using common household items. This activity works well as an inquiry-based lesson, one where you give students many supplies, give them a task, then let them use their own imagination to come up with something.

1. Ask students to make a list of items which float. Which of the things listed do they think could be used to make a boat?

2. Tell them their goal is to design and create a boat that will float. Divide students into groups of three or four. Have them create a list of materials they will need to make their boat. Have them bring in supplies from home, or provide supplies in class.

Here are some other ideas to try:

- Ivory soap floats! Give each student a bar of soap and a plastic knife. Have students use the knife to carve the soap into a boat.

- Give each student a 1' (30.48 cm) x 1' (30.48 cm) piece of aluminium foil. Help students bend and fold the foil into a boat that will float.

- Get a large chunk of used Styrofoam® from shipped packages, or from a craft store. Give students a plastic knife that will cut through the Styrofoam®. Ask students to create a boat that resembles the one May Amelia and her brothers use.

Once the boats are made, float them in tubs of water or in the sink. Try to get the boats to move across the water using the wind or a fan. (Note: You may use waterproof containers such as baking pans or plastic storage containers. These containers can also be used for the Fun Run activity on page 21.)

If your school is near a body of water, try floating the boats outdoors. Conduct short-distance races using stop-watches to time. Try placing objects in the boat to represent people and belongings. Do the objects make a difference relating to how fast or accurately the boats maneuver?

Is there a boating store or marine shipyard in your area? Is there a parent who is in the Navy? A boating specialist could make a presentation to your class on the evolution of boating technology.

Charting May Amelia's Roots

May has so many relatives that it may be hard to keep all the characters straight. Creating a family tree may help you visualize the relationships between the family members.

Complete May's family tree by filling in the chart below. Once you have completed the names, join together with a partner. In your partnership, decide on an adjective that best describes each character. Put the agreed-upon adjectives on the *dotted* lines beside the person's name. One name and adjective has already been completed on the chart.

Example: Grandmother Patience *cruel*

Pappa _____ Aunt Feenie _____ Aunt Aili _____

Alma _____ Uncle Henry _____ Uncle Asmus _____

Matti _____ Isaiah _____ Uncle Aarno _____

Wendell _____ Alvin _____ Aunt Saara _____

Ivan _____ Wilbert _____ Kaarlo _____

May _____ Amy _____ Aunt Alice _____

Where in the World Is May Amelia?

We know that the Jackson family lives in a Finnish settlement along the Nasel River. Where is the Nasel River? How close or far away would May Amelia live to you? Conduct the following research to find out.

1. If computers are available, log on and find a map of Washington State from the 1890s. Once there, conduct a search to find maps of Washington State. Type in "Washington State maps." If there are no computers, use an atlas from the library. Find the following real-life places that the fictional May lived in during the 1890s. You should be looking in the southwestern corner of the state.

   a. Locate Pacific County.   b. Locate the Nasel River.

2. Using the outline map below of Washington State:

   a. Make dotted lines showing the outline of Pacific County.

   b. Draw in the Nasel River.

   c. Label Astoria, Oregon.

   d. Label Knappton.

3. Compare your map to the map in the front of the novel.   Since Pacific County is actually a very small portion of Washington, you may want to draw a separate map consisting solely of an enlarged Pacific County. Add the following to the map.

   a. The Jackson farm   d. The Smith Island
   b. The Petersen farm   e. Thymei's cranberry bogs
   c. Armstrong Logging Camp

Family Matters

May feels closest to her brother Wilbert. He seems to be the one who understands her the most. He is the one she goes to when she is sad. In everyone's life, there is someone who has a strong, positive influence. Who in your life has shown you a special kind of friendship by acting lovingly to you in some way? Has this person risked something to help you? Did this person listen when you needed to talk? Has he/she made sacrifices for you? Who in your life do you feel most connected to? In the space below, write the person's name, his/her relation to you, and what this person has done for you.

One of the most wonderful things you can do for someone is to show appreciation. Write a letter to your friend or relative expressing thanks for what was done. Mention your gratitude and describe how this person's influence has helped you.

Remember, a friendly letter has a heading (return address and date), greeting, body, closing, and signature. Be sure to include all of these parts in your letter of thanks.

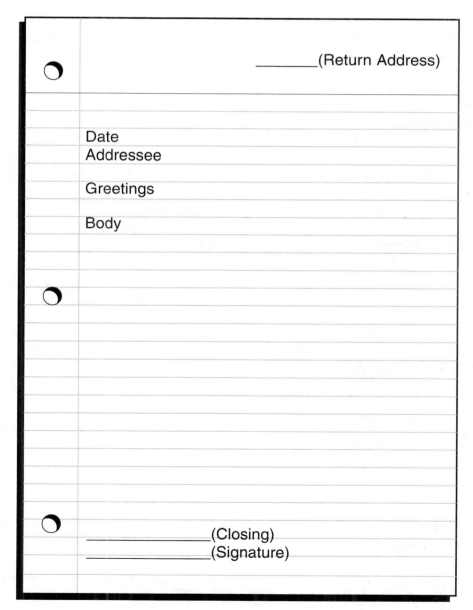

Quiz Time!

Answer the following questions from chapters 6 through 8.

1. What determines when the Jackson children return to school?

   _____

   _____

2. Why doesn't May want to be a "proper young lady"?

   _____

   _____

3. How is the community notified when the splash dam is going to be opened?

   _____

   _____

4. Describe the predicament May, Lonny, Kaarlo, and Wilbert find themselves in while they are crossing the bridge to the cranberry bogs.

   _____

   _____

5. What news about Matti does Uncle Aarno bring?

   _____

   _____

6. What idea does May come up with "to turn the bad luck around"?

   _____

   _____

7. How does May become stuck in a tree?

   _____

   _____

8. Where does May's mother give birth?

   _____

   _____

9. How is the baby named?

   _____

   _____

10. What types of tasks does May do for Baby Amy?

   _____

   _____

Fun Run

May Amelia must run from the mill to the downstream households to warn everyone that lumber is rapidly travelling down the river. She has to run fast enough to get to the houses before the logs do. How fast does she have to run in order to reach the people before the potentially deadly logs do?

Teacher note: Demonstrate the equation, *speed = distance ÷ time* in class.

Example: A boat can travel 20 miles in 80 minutes. What is the speed of the boat? Speed = 20 miles ÷ 80 minutes. Speed = .25 miles per minute

A copy of the story problems (below) should be given to each student. The details of the problems can be figured out together as a class, or individually, depending on students' levels of ability.

Materials:

- Waterproof, rectangular containers. Baking pans or plastic storage containers will work well. You will need one container for each group of students.
- Water (enough to fill each container about halfway)
- Unsharpened wooden pencils

Procedure:

Fill up the container with water and figure out a way to get the water to move the pencil(s) from one end of the container to the other end (i.e., tipping the container slightly, blowing on the pencil, or using a fan). If you time how long it takes the pencil to travel from one end to the other, and measure the length it travelled, you can use the $s = d \div t$ formula to figure out the average speed the pencil travelled "down the river."

Story Problems

1. May has to run one mile to reach the first house. She manages to run the mile in six minutes. What is the speed she ran? _____

2. The logs, travelling downstream, will reach the first house in ten minutes. We already know the first house is one mile away. What is the speed of the river?

   _____

3. Using the information given in problems 1 and 2, will May Amelia be able to out-run the logs? Answer in a complete sentence. _____

4. The river flows at a speed of ten miles per hour. If the logs travel downstream with the current and reach the second house in two hours, how many miles away is the second house?

   _____

5. Prepare the "river" as explained by your teacher. Using your teacher's explanation, figure out the speed the pencil travelled "down the river." Show all math work in the space below, using diagrams to help explain what you did.

   _____

Character Charades

This is a test to see how well you know the characters of *Our Only May Amelia*. You are going to play the game of charades. Cut out all the name strips below and place them in a hat. Select a name from the hat. The object of the game is to use body motions and facial expressions to get your classmates to guess who you are. You cannot talk or make any sounds. For example, if you are trying to get your classmates to guess Wendell, you might pretend that you are sewing with a needle and thread.

May Amelia	Kaarlo
Grandmother Patience	Miss. McEwing
Pappa	Alvin and Ivan
Baby Amy	Bosie
Mamma	Aunt Alice
the Crying Indian	Aunt Feenie
Wendell	Uncle Henry
Jane	Uncle Aarno
Wilbert	Mr. Clayton
Olaaf Kuula	Lonny Peterson
Matti	Ben Armstrong
Mrs. Peterson	

Gender Benders

The title of this novel emphasizes the fact that May Amelia is the only female child in a family of eight children. She has six brothers and one male cousin who live with her. The actual likelihood of this occurring is quite rare. Since she is "our only May Amelia," what is the probability that she would be the only girl-child in a family of seven children (not counting Kaarlo)?

Teacher note: Explain to students that probability is a measure of how likely it is that some event will occur. For your purposes in this lesson, suggest that there is aequal chance of having either a male or a female each time a child is born. Each birth event is also usually assumed to be "statistically independent" from the other, which means that just because a family has a daughter, they will not automatically have a son the next time. Ask students for examples from their own family to support this theory. (Note there are always exceptions!)

Students should be able to calculate the likelihood of a family having two children, one boy and one girl. First the students should be shown how to count the total number possible number of events that can occur. The following event tree for a boy and a girl family illustrates that there are four possible events:

Event	First Child	Second Child	Event
#1	Boy	Boy	1/4 or 25%
#2	Boy	Girl	1/4 or 25%
#3	Girl	Boy	1/4 or 25%
#4	Girl	Girl	1/4 or 25%

You can see from the chart that there are four distinct possibilities. To calculate the probability of a family having a boy and a girl, look at the table, count the number of boy/girl events, and add the probabilities to each event. In the two-child family example, the probability of having a boy and a girl is $\frac{1}{4} + \frac{1}{4} = \frac{1}{2}$, which is also 50%.

Now challenge the students to calculate the liklihood of a family of five children having one male and four female children. Ask the students to create an event tree. They should conclude that, in a five child family, their are 32 possible family types. Since the male could have been born first, second, third, fourth or fifth, five of these 32 events have only one boy. Consequently, the probability of a one boy/four girl family is $\frac{1}{32} + \frac{1}{32} + \frac{1}{32} + \frac{1}{32} + \frac{1}{32} = \frac{5}{32}$, which is 15.6%

Pass out the following problems to students. Let them work in pairs to work through the problems. Some students may have trouble understanding the math. After they have tried to figure out the problems for a little while, you may want to work on the problems as a class.

1. Mathematically figure out the probability of there being one female child and six male children in the same family.
2. Write a paragraph explaining how May's probability (i.e., problem 1) was computed.
3. Create and solve another gender probability problem using your own family.
4. Write a paragraph explaining the male/female ratio of the family you chose to use/create for question 3.
5. If May Amelia's mother has an eighth child, what are the odds of that child being a female?

Mixed Up Names

May Amelia is so excited when her mother gives birth to a baby girl. She becomes more enthused when her mother allows her to name the baby. May names the baby Amy, because it's "May all mixed up."

- Can you create any other names by mixing up the letters of your first name? You do not have to use all the letters.

  _____   _____

  _____   _____

- Try combining the letters of your first and last name. What other names are hidden in your full name?

  _____   _____

  _____   _____

- Are you having trouble making names out of your own name? See who can come up with the most words by using the letters in students' full names.

- Use a dictionary to find a very long word that begins with the same letter as your first name. For example, if your name begins with an "A," look in the "A" section in the dictionary. What is a long word in the dictionary that begins with "A"?

- Use a baby naming book to look up your name. What other names does the book say are similar to your name? What does your name mean? Where does it originate from? What other forms of your name would you like to be called? Is there anything that may be a shorter version of your name that you could use as a nickname?

- There are some internet sites that function the same as a baby naming book. Type in the key words "baby names" and see where it takes you. Look for a site which will allow you to type in any name for its meaning and origin.

- Some web sites have name popularity graphs. You type in any name, and it will show you during what decade the name originated in, and the popularity of the name throughout the decades. What were the most popular female and male names given to babies during the year you were born? Do any of the names that are popular surprise you? What names seem to be most common in your school or area? What are some common names for mothers, fathers, and grandparents of students in your class?

- Conduct research to find out how your school or town got its name.

Quiz Time!

Answer the following questions from chapters 9 and 10.

1. Describe the mood of Chapter 9 as it begins.

   _____

   _____

2. What happens to Baby Amy?

   _____

   _____

3. What does Grandmother Patience accuse May Amelia of doing?

   _____

   _____

4. Why does May think she is in heaven when she wakes up in Astoria?

   _____

   _____

5. Why does May Amelia's father allow May and Wilbert to stay at Aunt Feenie's house?

   _____

   _____

6. How does the number of men compare with the number of women who live in Astoria?

   _____

   _____

7. How does Mariah differ from the stories May has heard about her?

   _____

   _____

8. Why do Alvin and Ivan get upset with May?

   _____

   _____

9. What occurs that creates a potential danger for travel by boat?

   _____

   _____

10. How does May stop her stubborn twin brothers from getting on the boat?

   _____

   _____

Self-Scrap

To coincide with the Keeping Track of Baby activity on page 29, have students bring in some recent photocopied pictures of themselves, their families, and/or friends. Each student will create a scrapbook page to be put together, in order to make up an entire bulletin board display and/or a photo album.

Materials:

- An 8½" (21.6 cm) x 11" (27.9 cm) or 1' (30.48 cm) x 1' (30.48 cm) piece of thick paper or cardstock for every student in the class
- regular scissors
- glue
- decorative scissors such as pinking shears (optional)
- assorted pieces of colored cardstock or construction paper
- stickers, magazines, or computer graphics
- photo album (optional)

Procedure:

Give each student a background piece of thick paper, cardstock, or a special page out of a scrapbook that is either 8½" x 11" or 12" x 12". These are the typical sizes for scrapbooks or photo albums. This initial paper will serve as the background of a photo album page.

Students will need to make a matte around their photos using different colors of paper or cardstock. Mattes are made by first trimming the photo to the desired size and shape. Use a glue stick to adhere the photo onto a piece of colored paper. Trim the colored paper around the photo so there is a ¼" or ½" border of colored paper showing around all edges of the photograph. If you have fancy scissors such as pinking shears, you could also use these to trim the colored paper around the photo. Help students arrange the pictures on their background paper in several different ways before gluing them down permanently. Experiment by putting some on an angle and some straight.

Encourage students to use magazine cutouts, stickers, or clip art images to embellish their scrap book pages. You can buy all types of things at a local craft store, but most students will have things from home that they can bring in. Graphic programs on computers can also provide a wide variety of images that can be printed free of charge.

Hang the completed pages on a bulletin board. When the bulletin board is ready to be taken down, put the scrapbook pages together to make an entire album. Save it to display at your school's Open House celebration or at an end-of-the-year party.

Puppet Masters

May Amelia is often told that she is not a "proper lady." For someone who doesn't seem to be interested in feminine things, she loves her dolls! May's rag doll, Susannah, and her china doll, Baby Feenie, both get a lot of attention from the family.

In this activity, you will make a doll and use it in a puppet show.

Teacher Note: You will need to write various scenes on slips of paper then put the paper pieces into a hat so they can be selected randomly. Choose the scenes from below or use some from the Conversations on page 45. You will also need to designate an area to be used for a puppet show.

Here are some scenes that would work well as puppet shows:

- Wilbert finding May on Baby Island
- May, Wilbert, Alvin, and Ivan's trip to Astoria
- May's dessert experience in Astoria
- May and Isaiah at the Chinook funeral
- May and Kaarlo in the pigpen
- Kaarlo learning the truth about his parents and siblings

- Grandmother Patience's request for the perfect cup of tea
- May, Kaarlo, Wilbert, and Lonny running into a cougar
- May getting caught up the tree with the mamma bear below
- Alvin and Ivan coming to visit May and Wilbert in Astoria
- May going to her first dance

Materials:

- Socks and buttons or felt, needle and thread or glue
- Tongue depressors or craft sticks, colored paper or felt and glue
- Paper bags and markers, colored paper or felt and glue
- Sequins, feathers, beads, fabric scraps, stickers, yarn as needed

Procedure:

1. Design and create puppets of each character needed. You may choose to make sock puppets, puppets on tongue depressors, paper bag puppets, or any other type you can think of.

2. Put students into small groups. Ask a selected student in each to pick a scene from the book out of a hat, or use a scene from the list above.

3. Decide which characters are necessary for each particular scene.

4. Using the book, write a script to be used for a puppet show.

5. Rehearse the scene, then act it out for the class.

6. As a follow-up activity, you may want to perform your puppet skits to a group of small children, or arrange to perform at a local library.

Endangered Wolves

In 1899, Ben Armstrong's logging camp was probably set up and operated without any thoughts of the dangers that logging can do to the environment. These days, people are more concerned with the negative effects of logging. One of the environmental hazards is the decline of the Algonquin wolf population. Because of the deterioration of forests, these creatures are forced to exist in isolated populations. This limits the genetic diversity of the species. A limited genetic diversity may cause the wolves to become extinct. Using the Internet or encyclopedias, conduct research about the decline in the wolf population. Answer the following questions.

1. In what regions of the world have wolf populations already been eliminated?

   _____
   _____
   _____

2. Where would you find the healthiest wolf population in the world?

   _____
   _____
   _____

3. Are wolves harmful to humans?

   _____
   _____
   _____

4. If wolf populations decrease, what effects will this have on other species of animals who share the forest with them?

   _____
   _____
   _____

5. Because the wolves' population has declined, scientists have noticed some drastic changes in how wolves behave around other wolves. Describe one way that social wolf behavior has changed.

   _____
   _____
   _____

6. Do you feel it is more upsetting that wolves are killed by ignorant humans who think they are a threat, or that they are killed because of industry taking over their space? Explain your answer.

   _____
   _____
   _____

Keeping Track of Baby

May Amelia is so excited when her new baby sister is born! She is no longer the only girl on the Nasel. Since her mother is ill after giving birth, May takes it upon herself to keep track of baby Amy's "record" book. Nowadays, we call this record book a "baby book."

Encourage students to request a baby book from their parents. Some students may not be able to obtain a book, but they might collect early pictures or other memorabilia that serves as a record of their younger years.

1. Hold a show-and-tell day for early childhood books, pictures, and other items. Teachers can participate, as well!

2. Collect baby pictures from faculty members. Post pictures on a bulletin board and play "guess that baby." Award a prize for the student who guesses the most correct pictures.

3. Either of these activities might inspire a writing assignment. Below, ask students to describe the most memorable item from their childhood, or to compare Amy Jackson's baby record with their own baby book.

Answer the following questions

1. What is May's first female

   _____   _____

   _____   _____

2. What important secret does Aunt Alice share with May and Emma?

   _____

   _____

3. What does Otto say would happen to a "Chinaman" if he broke the law?

   _____

   _____

4. Why does May's father come and insist that May and Wilbert return home?

   _____

   _____

5. How do May and Wilbert show their friendship towards Lonny?

   _____

   _____

6. What three things does Jane give to May and Wilbert?

   _____

   _____

7. Describe the condition of the Peterson house when May and Wilbert go to visit Lonny.

   _____

   _____

8. When May and Wilbert invite Lonny and Mr. Peterson for supper, what happens at the table that puts Pappa in an "ornery mood"?

   _____

   _____

9. Why does May want to go to Smith Island?

   _____

   _____

10. What is surprising about Pappa's reaction when he sees that May is safe?

    _____

    _____

Using Chopsticks

The Chinese and other Asian cultures use chopsticks in the same way that other cultures use forks. May Amelia has a difficult time using chopsticks at Otto's house. In this activity, you will try to pick up various items from bowls using chopsticks. See if you are more coordinated than May!

Materials:

- Several pairs of chopsticks

- Bowls

- Assorted items to be picked up with chopsticks (such as markers, marbles, pencils, paper clips, and cooked rice)

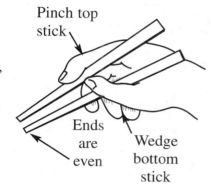

Procedure:

Discuss chop stick etiquette. Never spear food with chopsticks, never use only a single chopstick to eat, do not use two hands when using chopsticks, and always rest chopsticks on special holders—never in or across the bowl.

To use chopsticks, hold both sticks in one hand. Rest the end of one chopstick in the V between your thumb and pointer finger. Support the chopstick with your pinkie and ring finger. Hold the upper stick like you would hold a pencil, between your middle finger and your pointer finger, anchored down with your thumb. Make sure the ends of the chopsticks are always even with each other. If one chopstick protrudes longer than the other, it will become virtually impossible to use them effectively. When picking up food, only the upper chopstick (one held like a pencil) moves. The lower chopstick (one in the V of your thumb and forefinger) always remains still.

Place assorted items in the bowls and try to pick the items up using chopsticks. Put progressively more difficult items in each bowl, the most difficult being marbles.

Discuss the idea that people of varied cultures use different utensils for eating. Brainstorm, then use the chart below to record the different foods you can eat with varied utensils. Beside each utensil, list the foods for which it might be used.

UTENSIL	FOOD
Forks	
Spoons	
Knives	
Chopsticks	
Straws	
Fingers	
Other	

Journal Sharing

Select a few journal entries from your collection of entries that you would not mind sharing with a classmate. Your teacher will pair you up with another student. Once paired, choose a specific journal entry on the same topic that you both want to share.

Read each other's journal entry. Then re-read your own journal entry, written on the same topic as your friend's entry. By combining the information written in both journal entries, you are going to write an informal letter to May Amelia. Be sure to tell May how you feel about the topic and how your friend feels, too.

Here is a sample letter to May Amelia for a journal topic from Chapter 1.

Journal topic: May Amelia is the "only" girl in her family, and in fact the only young girl in the entire settlement. How does she feel about being the "only" girl? Write about a situation in which you have been the "only" someone or something.

Dear May,

It certainly must be hard for you to be the only girl in the Nasel. You must feel so alone at times, and that no one understands you. I do not blame you for trying to act like "one of the boys." After all, you have never seen what other girls do. The only way you know how to act is like a boy. It is unfortunate that Pappa does not understand this.

I can sympathize with you for being the "only" something. I have never been the only female in a situation, but I was the only non-Jewish person at a day camp one year. You see, my mother's boss was Jewish. He said he would pay for my sister and I to go to camp that summer, but only if we went to the Jewish Day Camp. I felt very awkward and alone at first. It didn't take me long to realize that we were still all the same, just kids who like to do the same things. There were some religious aspects to the camp, and I learned a lot from it.

My friend Carl has found himself in a predicament where he is the "only" something too. He is the only Hispanic person in his Art class. For the first few weeks, he felt like everyone was looking at him weirdly. They wondered if he could understand the English that the teacher was speaking. Some people even spoke to him really slowly, like he was a little kid. Then, when everyone realized Carl could speak English and Spanish, they became very interested in him. They wanted to know how to say certain things in Spanish.

I hope things come around for you, just like they have for Carl and me.

Sincerely,

Kathryn Smith and Carl Sanchez

Telephone Translations

May Amelia becomes friends with an interesting person named Otto. Otto is able to carry on a conversation with May in Finnish and with the "Chinaman" in Chinese, simultaneously. You are going to play the childhood game of "Telephone" with a twist. Use the chart to select your phrases. Good luck!

Directions:

1. Arrange four students per group in a row.

2. The first person whispers a phrase from the list in English to the second person.

3. The second person has to translate the same phrase from English into Finnish to repeat to the third person.

4. The third person then translates what he/she heard in Finnish to Chinese. The phrase is then whispered in Chinese to the fourth person.

5. The fourth person in the row has to translate from Chinese back to English and say the phrase out loud. The first person can check for accuracy.

6. All four people then rotate positions and start the process over with another phrase.

English	Finnish	Chinese
hello	hei	ni hao
good morning	hyvaa huomenta	zao shang hao
good evening	hyvaa iltaa	wan shang hao
good night	hyvaa yota	wàn an
sorry	olen pahoillani	duì bu qu
thank you	kiitos	xiè xie
How are you?	Mita kuuluu?	Ni hao ma?
yes	kylla	shì
no	ei	bù shì

Similarities and Differences

Originally, you may have thought that you had nothing in common with a 19th Century Finnish-American girl who lived in a settlement in Washington state. After reading the book, you may have found that you and May Amelia are actually very similar, or perhaps you still feel very different from her. Use the Venn diagram to compare and contrast yourself to May.

> **Teacher note:** You may ask students to compare and contrast themselves to different characters, as well.

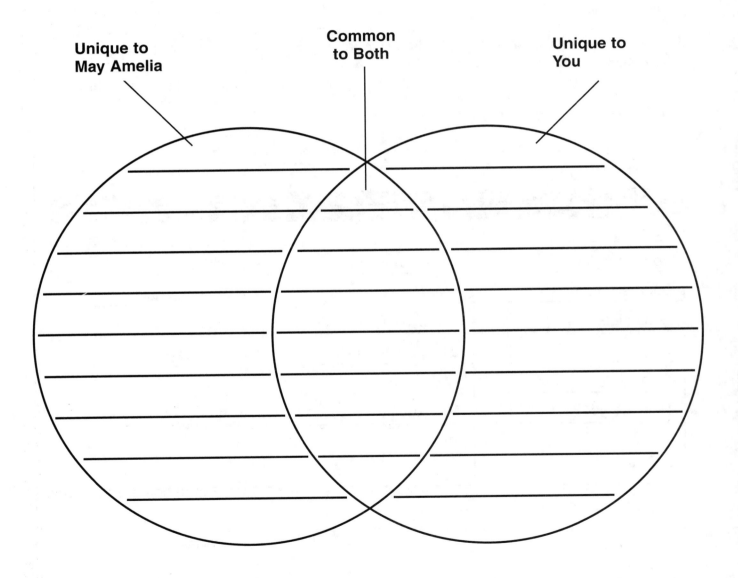

Unique to May Amelia

Common to Both

Unique to You

Any Questions?

Now that you have finished reading *Our Only May Amelia*, are there any questions that are left unanswered? Write three of your questions here.

_____

_____

_____

_____

_____

Working alone, in pairs, or in small groups, prepare possible answers for the questions you have asked above and those written below. When you have finished your predictions, share your ideas with the class.

- Does May Amelia's mother ever have any more children? If so, will May Amelia ever get another sister?

- What might have caused Amy to die? Why did she cough so much?

- Does May's father ever find out the truth about Matti and Mary O' Casey?

- Will they ever hear from Matti again?

- Will Matti and Mary be accepted if they bring grandchildren home to the Jackson family?

- Will May Amelia ever become lady-like?

- Will she ever get married and have children of her own?

- Will May Amelia ever get to travel around the world like she envisions?

- Do things ever get better for the Jackson family?

- Does May ever see Emma and Otto again after she goes back home?

- Does Kaarlo ever become more pleasant?

- Describe the relationship between May and her father. Does Pappa come around and learn to accept May for who she is?

- Does May mature and realize that Pappa will never change his views?

- Does Wendell ever become a doctor?

- Do any other Jackson children go off to obtain more schooling?

Book Report Ideas

There are many ways to report on a book once it has been read. After you have finished *Our Only May Amelia,* choose a method of reporting on it that appeals to you. It may be an idea of your own or one of the suggestions listed below.

Come to Life—A size-appropriate group prepares a scene from the story for dramatization, acts it out, and relates the significance of the scene to the entire book. Costumes and props will add to the dramatization!

Into the Future—Predict what might happen if *Our Only May Amelia* were to continue. You may write it as a story in narrative form or a dramatic script, or create a visual display.

A Character Comes to Life—Suppose one of the characters in *Our Only May Amelia* came to life and walked into your home or classroom. This report gives the character's point of view as he or she sees, hears, feels, and experiences the 21st century world in which you live. Dress up like the character to present your report.

Coming Attraction—*Our Only May Amelia* is about to be made into a movie and you have been chosen to design the promotional poster. Include the title and author of the book, a listing of the main characters and the contemporary actors who will play them, a drawing of a scene from the book, and a paragraph synopsis of the story that will make audiences want to see the movie.

Literary Interview—This report is done in pairs. One student will pretend to be a character in the story, assuming that character's persona. The other student will play the role of a radio or television interviewer, providing the audience with insights into the character's personality and life. It is the responsibility of both partners to create meaningful questions and appropriate answers.

Dust Jacket Design—Design a dust jacket for the novel, including the title, author, an important scene, image, or character on the cover, a book summary on the inside flaps, and a teaser (a hint at the plot that will make people want to read the book).

Radio Review—Write a radio script reviewing *Our Only May Amelia.* Find suitable background music and use a "radio broadcasting voice" to tape your program.

Letter It—Write a letter to a family member or friend. In the letter, summarize the novel and tell why you would or would not recommend reading it.

Diorama Display—Create a diorama representing your favorite part or most significant scene in the book. Position it in the classroom or school library for other students to see.

Trading Cards—Create trading cards for characters in *Our Only May Amelia.* Draw the character's face and name on the front. On the back of the card, give information about the character. You may have to make up some information, such as exact date of births. Use the list of characters found on page 22.

Research Ideas

Describe three things that you read in *Our Only May Amelia* that you would like to learn more about.

1. _____

2. _____

3. _____

As you read *Our Only May Amelia*, you encountered many geographic locations, true-to-life people, Finnish customs and lifestyles, and superstitions. To increase your understanding of the characters and events in the book, as well as to appreciate Jennifer Holm as a writer, research to find out more about these people, places, and things.

Work in groups to research one or more of the areas you named above or those listed below. Share your findings with the rest of the class in any appropriate format for oral presentation.

- logging:

  —affects on wildlife

  —affects on water pollution

  —affects on forest fires

- Oscar Wirkkala

- brain damage

- Finnish uses for saunas

- Scarlet fever

- pasteurization

- Washington state

- Chinook customs

- gillnetters

- Nasel River

- Finnish proverbs

- dysentery

- salmon

- herbal remedies

- tanning hides

- Finnish meals

- Lutherans

- China

- stages of grief

- Astoria

- Finnish and Irish dislike for one another

News on the Nasel

By now, you probably have a very good picture of what it was like to live in a settlement on the Nasel River in 1899. Transportation had to be accomplished by walking or rowing a boat. Due to the limited means of transportation, communication was slow. Receiving mail or newspapers was rare. That certainly did not mean that there was no news to be told on the Nasel! May and her family had many newsworthy adventures and experiences.

You are going to create a full newspaper detailing the happenings of May and her family as they occurred throughout the book. Every student should turn at least one of their journal entries into a newspaper article. Several of these entries can easily be reworded to be letters to the editor, obituaries, or current news events.

To plan what the whole newspaper should include, get into groups of three or four and use the following page to brainstorm ideas. Each member of the group should also decide on which section they would like to work. Nominate a spokesperson to present your group's ideas to the whole class. As a class, combine the brainstormed information and choose the sections of the newspaper that will be included. Create sub-committees of people who elected to work on specific sections. Also choose the news topics that should be covered. News stories can be slightly embellished, as long as they are based on actual occurrences in the novel.

Here are some (embellished) sample headlines of events that occurred in chapters 1–3 in the book. See what you can come up with for the remainder of the novel.

Crazy Man Arrested for Attempted Murder of Twins

Fierce Smell Coming from Pier

Logger Loses Leg in a Freak Accident: Are the Woods Cursed?

The Only Girl on the Nasel

News on the Nasel *(cont.)*

Each small group should have a copy of this page to use for the News on the Nasel activity. Use your Reader's Response Journal entries to come up with the articles.

Brainstorm Sheet

Members of group and preferred section (Example: Johnny = Letters to Editor):

Parts of newspaper that should be included:

Section 1 possible headlines of articles:

Section 2 possible headlines of articles:

Section 3 possible headlines of articles:

Section 4 possible headlines of articles:

Section 5 possible headlines of articles:

Finnish Settlement Party

Why not invite your family or another class to your room to learn more about what life was like on a Finnish settlement at the turn of the century?

Students will enjoy planning, preparing for, and participating in their own party.

Party Checklist

Three weeks before the party . . .

❑ Decide when and where the party will occur.

❑ Discuss how you will incorporate the Finnish theme into your party. Will you have food to sample (such as Laksloda on page 11)? Will you appear in costumes? Will you display some of your boats (page 16), puppets (page 27), or scrapbook pages you made (page 26) while reading the novel? Will you play Finnish music? Maybe you'll play the Finnish game of Kyykkä (page 42).

❑ Talk about whom you want to invite. Perhaps you'll want to invite younger students. You may want to invite parents or other family members. Make and send invitations (page 41).

Two weeks before the party . . .

❑ Pass around a sign-up sheet. Each student should be encouraged to contribute something unique to the party. They might bring food, sign up to make a display on logging camps, read a poem in Finnish, or demonstrate a Finnish game.

❑ Send home a note to students' parents to remind them of the party, and to let them know what students signed up to bring.

One week before the party . . .

❑ Send home a note reminding students of what they are to bring for the party.

❑ Buy and/or make decorations.

❑ Decide what food and drink you will make as a class. Make a grocery list.

The day before the party . . .

❑ Make food and prepare drinks.

The day of the party . . .

❑ Decorate the party space and set up stations needed for the activities that are going to occur.

Enjoy!

Finnish Settlement Party *(cont.)*

Come to a Finnish Settlement Party!

Day:

Time:

Place:

Hosts:

Theme:

The Game of Kyykkä

Play a game similar to an authentic Finnish game at your party! Kyykkä is an old Finnish game similar to several games of the kind played throughout Europe, beginning in the Middle Ages.

Object of the Game

Kyykkä is played with two teams of four players each. The object of the original game is for each team to try to empty the other team's playing court of kyykkä pieces, or pins, by throwing a stick or club. The first team that manages to knock out all the other team's pins wins the game. In this version of the game, use beanbags or soft handballs, to make it safer for children to play. You can divide your class down the middle to make two teams.

Equipment

Each team requires 20 pins. The pins were originally wooden cylinders. For this version, use empty soda cans or plastic juice bottles. You need enough beanbags or handballs for one team. Mark off an area in a field or parking lot that has two 20' x 13' (6m x 4m) playing courts between which there is a 23′ (7m) space. The longest sides of each court face each other. Use tape or chalk to mark off the court area.

Rules of the Game

Each team arranges their 20 cans in an evenly-spaced row on the front edge of their court. (The front edge is the one closest to the 23' space.) The players throw their balls from inside their own court.

To begin, Team One players throw their beanbags or balls into Team Two's court, trying to knock the opposing teams' cans out of the court. Meanwhile, Team Two stands outside the court away from where the beanbags or balls are being thrown. When the bags or balls have been thrown, Team Two retrieves them, and then throws them into Team One's court, trying to knock out their cans. Players on Team One then retrieve their beanbags or balls.

The game continues until all the cans belonging to one team are outside of the court. The first team to knock the other team's cans out of the court wins!

Objective Test and Essay

Matching: Match these quotes with the characters who said them.

May	Mamma	Grandmother Patience
Wilbert	Pappa	

1. "Children must learn to speak English or else [they] will always have trouble."

   _____

2. "No good's gonna come of [May Amelia] looking after the babe. This girl doesn't have the sense that God gave her." _____

3. "May Amelia Jackson, don't you give up on me, you hear me May, I am not about to stand for it, you come back to yourself and me." _____

4. "Cause I don't want to lose anyone else, not even a pair of stubborn brothers I've missed every day." _____

5. "This will keep you warm my little May. After all, you're the only May we've got."

   _____

True or False: Answer true or false in the blanks below.
1. May Amelia's mother and her Aunt Alice are similar. _____
2. According to Chinnook legend, when an owl hoots it means that the harvest is going to be bad.
3. May cuts her hair because she wants a job at the logging camp. _____
4. May realizes the stories she has heard about Mariah are false once she meets her and spends time with her. _____
5. May doesn't go to Grandmother Patience's funeral because she is still in Astoria.

   _____

Short Answer: Provide a short answer for each of these questions.
1. Why does May refer to herself as "a no-good girl"?_____

   _____

2. How did Kaarlo come to live with the Jacksons? _____

   _____

3. What does Wilbert mean when he says that "Grandmother Patience was poorly named." _____

   _____

4. Why are May and Wilbert allowed to stay at Aunt Feenie's house?_____

   _____

5. Why does Wilbert say, "I bet Lonny's feeling a whole lot worse than you May."? _____

   _____

Essay: Respond to the following on a separate sheet of paper.
1. Jennifer Holm begins the novel with a Finnish proverb that reads: "If you don't go, you can't return." How does this saying apply to May Amelia from a literal (or physical) standpoint throughout the book? How does it apply to her from an emotional standpoint? Provide at least two examples from the book.

2. By now, you have spent a lot of time getting to know the Jackson family. If you were growing up in May Amelia's family, which family member do you think you would be? Explain why and how are you most like this Jackson.

Response

Explain the meaning of these quotations from *Our Only May Amelia*.

Teacher Note: Choose the appropriate number of quotes to which your students should respond.

Chapter 1   "Children must learn to speak English or else we will always have trouble."

Chapter 1   "Children, I sure do hope your mama gives us another boy 'cause I don't think I can stand another May Amelia."

Chapter 2   "There ain't no gentlemen on the Nasel. Just a bunch of no-good brothers."

Chapter 3   "You hafta go May," "Wilbert says. "It's not every day that Isaiah prefers your company to the sheep's."

Chapter 3   "There's bad blood in the very ground guarantee my words, I once found an elk all gutted up no heart there at all or eyes either and its blood was drawn all over the trees. No wolf or bear can paint blood on trees."

Chapter 4   "She is beautiful but Pappa wouldn't like her because she's not a Finn . I have to keep it a secret."

Chapter 4   "He's not likely to forget that he's not a brother with you constantly reminding him, May."

Chapter 5   "Grandmother Patience was poorly named."

Chapter 6   "Mamma is a lady but not the usual kind."

Chapter 7   "Your fool of a brother Matti was at Mariah's tavern last night in Astoria and now he's gone missing. Shanghaied."

Chapter 8   "No good's gonna come of her looking after the babe. This girl doesn't have the sense that God gave her. Why, look at her."

Chapter 9   "May Amelia Jackson, don't you give up on me, you hear me May, I am not about to stand for it, you come back to yourself and me."

Chapter 10   "Cause I don't want to lose anyone else, not even a pair of stubborn brothers I've missed every day."

Chapter 11   "May Amelia Jackson, "Emma says," you are hopeless."

Chapter 12   "I truly thought I would never want to see the Nasel or our homestead again. But as we row up the Nasel, the familiar sight of our house nestled in the valley with the great mountains rising around it makes my heart beat faster."

Chapter 13   "I bet Lonny's feeling a whole lot worse than you May."

Conversations

Work in size-appropriate groups to write and perform the conversation that might have occurred in one of the following situations. If you prefer, you may use your own conversation idea for characters from *Our Only May Amelia*.

- Pappa tells May that he doesn't want her near the logging camp because she is a girl. *(2 people)*

- Wilbert tries to make May feel better at Baby Island. *(two people)*

- Aunt Alice tells Mamma that she has had enough children. *(three people)*

- May convinces her brothers to let her fire the shotgun. *(four people)*

- Ivan and Alvin put gravy on May's dessert. *(five people)*

- May and Isaiah witness the Chinook funeral and May is brought home by the Crying Indian. *(four people)*

- Isaiah apologizes to May and brings her kittens. *(three people)*

- An older girl questions May about where Matti is. *(two people)*

- May knocks Kaarlo in the muddy pig pen "by accident." *(three people)*

- Kaarlo finds out the truth about his family. *(three people)*

- May convinces Kaarlo to come home. *(two people)*

- Grandmother Patience demands a cup of tea. *(two people)*

- Miss McEwing talks to May and Wilbert about why they have not been in school. *(three people)*

- May convinces Lars to let her run and give the log warning. *(two people)*

- Pappa shows May how to feed the baby with cow milk. *(eight people)*

- May and Wilbert meet the true Mariah. *(three people)*

- Alvin and Ivan insist that they are getting on the Gleaner, until May steps in. *(five people)*

- Emma and May discuss boys. *(two people)*

- Aunt Alice discusses eloping with May and Emma. *(three people)*

- Pappa tells May that Grandmother Patience has died. *(four people)*

Bibliography

Children's Literature (with related content)

Angell, Judie. *One-Way to Ansonia.* Simon and Schuster, 1985.

Collidge, Olivia. *Come by Here.* Wiley & Sons, 2002.

Duffy, James. *Radical Red.* Simon and Schuster, 1993.

Durbin, William. *The Journal of Otto Peltonen, A Finnish Immigrant.* Scholastic, 2000.

Jansson, Tove. *Comet in Moominland.* Avon Books, 1959.

Jansson, Tove. *Moominpappa at Sea.* Avon Books, 1966.

Fleischman, Sid. *Jim Ugly.* Dell, 1992.

Hill, Pamela. *Ghost Horses.* Turtleback Books, 1999.

Kilpatrick, Katherine. *Keeping the Good Light.* Laurel Leaf, 1999.

Pullman, Phillip. *Ruby in the Smoke.* Scholastic, 1999.

Reid, Van. *Cordelia Underwood.* Van Reid, 1998.

Voight, Cynthia. *Calendar Papers.* H.W. Wilson, 1983.

References and Teacher Resources

Lander, Patricia, and Claudette Charbonneau. *The Land and People of Finland.* J.P. Lippincott, 1990

McNair, Sylvia. *Finland, Enchantment of the World.* Grolier, 1997

Ojakangas, Beatrice. *The Finnish Cookbook.* Crown, 1977

Web Sites

What you need to know about Geography—*http://www.geography.about.com*

Wildlands League—*www.wildlandsleague.org*

Answer Key

Page 10
1. Accept all reasonable answers.
2. May is the only female child in the family, and the only girl her age in the entire settlement.
3. Wilbert seems to understand May the most and looks out for her.
4. May feels like she is "a no-good girl" because she is always getting into trouble with her father for not acting lady-like.
5. Wilbert thinks Baby Island is cursed because that is where the Chinooks bury their dead and there are spirits wandering around.
6. May and Wilbert go to Astoria to shop for her mother.
7. They stop along the way at Lonny Peterson's house to say hello, then near Olaaf Kuula's farm to let May shoot the shotgun, before going to Astoria.
8. The twins put gravy on her dessert, allowing May to think it is fresh-whipped cream.
9. Astoria is very different from the Nasel Settlement. The houses are fancier than farmhouses, there are Chinamen on the docks, there are sailors and fishermen everywhere, and there are strange new odors coming from the cannery.
10. Aunt Alice has a polished appearance, with neat hair and a silk dress. She is "less Finnish" because she speaks English and cooks English food. She does not have a husband, but entertains a "gentleman friend."

Page 15
1. May is a miracle because she is the only girl in a family of boys.
2. Isaiah and May witness the funeral of a Chinook mother and infant.
3. The Crying Indian helps May.
4. Matti has a secret Irish girlfriend.
5. May drops the board as Kaarlo is about to hammer it, which causes Kaarlo to fall in the mud.
6. Kaarlo is actually a cousin who had to stay with the Jacksons

because his family couldn't afford his travel expenses. His family has died of the "fever."
7. The family feels terribly sad when Kaarlo leaves because they know his heart is broken.
8. Grandmother Patience tries to change where she will be sleeping, the cohabitation of May and Wilbert, the furniture, and May Amelia's personality.
9. When Wilbert learns that May has been hurt by Grandmother Patience, he sneaks in during the night and steals her cane.
10. Grandmother Patience is not happy with May to begin with, then May can't get her tea perfectly hot or sweet for her. She smashes the doll to pieces to hurt May.

Page 20
1. The Jackson children cannot go to school until the harvest is in.
2. May does not think that being a "proper young lady" is fun.
3. When the splash dam opens, a child is sent to run down the river to warn everyone that the logs are coming.
4. May, her brothers, and Lonny run into a cougar on the bridge.
5. Uncle Aarno tells the Jacksons that Matti has been shanghaied.
6. May thinks she can catch Micah Anderson.
7. May gets stuck in a tree because she is running from the mother bear.
8. May's mother gives birth in the Petersons' sauna.
9. May gets to name the baby since she is the only sister. She names her Amy, because it is "May all mixed up."
10. May takes care of Amy. She feeds her and keeps a baby record book for her.

Page 21
1. Speed = 1 mile/6 minutes
   Speed = 0.16 miles per minute
2. Speed = 1 mile/10 minutes
   Speed = 0.10 miles per minute
3. May is running faster than the river is flowing.

4. 10 mph = distance / 2 hours
   distance = 20 miles
5. Use same formula, plug in the numbers obtained, and then solve.

Page 23
1. (1/128) 7 = 7/128 or 5.46%
2. Their are a total of 128 combinations for seven children. Seven combinations will produce six boys and one girl. So 1/128 + 1/128 + 1/128 + 1/128 + 1/128 + 1/128 + 1/128 = 7/128 or 5.46%
3. Accept all logical problems.
4. Answers will vary based on problem created.
5. There is a 50/50 chance of getting a boy or a girl, regardless of what the gender is of the previous children.

Page 25
1. The mood of the beginning of chapter nine is sad.
2. Baby Amy has died.
3. Grandmother Patience says that Amy's death is May's fault.
4. May thinks she is in heaven because it is so warm, there is someone talking to her in a nice voice, and the bed she is in was "glorious."
5. Pappa feels badly that May is upset. He does not want to make things worse for her, so he allows her and Wilbert to stay in Astoria.
6. There are not many females in Astoria, but there are many men because it is a fishermen's town.
7. Mariah is not an evil person, and doesn't seem like the type to have someone shanghaied. She also does not keep money tucked in her leg, and is always helpful to others.
8. Alvin and Ivan get upset with May because she refuses to go home with them and acts as if she does not even miss them.

Answer Key (cont.)

Page 25 (cont.)

9. The river freezes, making travel by boat very dangerous.
10. May stops the twins from getting on the boat by telling them that she cares about them and doesn't want to lose them.

Page 28

1. Wolf populations have been eliminated from many European and Asian countries, Mexico, and most of the lower 48 United States.
2. Canada has the healthiest wolf population.
3. Wolves fear humans and do not see them as prey. There is no documentation of a human ever being killed by a wolf in North America.
4. When wolf populations decrease, the population of their prey increases. There will be an increase in the amount of moose and deer, which can cause damaging affects on tree populations. If tree populations decrease, then the food web of the forest is disrupted.
5. Wolves used to hunt in packs; now they are beginning to hunt alone or in pairs. They used to reuse dens for their pups for several years, and now they are not reusing the same areas.
6. Accept all reasonable opinions.

Page 30

1. May's friend Emma is interested in boys and is considered a "proper young lady."
2. Aunt Alice tells May and Emma that Matti eloped.
3. Otto says a Chinaman would not be able to get in trouble too easily, because no one can tell who is who.
4. May's father comes to get May and Wilbert because Grandmother Patience has died and Wendell is very sick.
5. May and Wilbert bring Lonny a pie.
6. Jane gives May and Wilbert Yiu-yu sweat, a Chinook dress for Susannah, and a black feather.
7. The Peterson house is a mess. The only room that is clean is Mr. and Mrs. Peterson's room.
8. Mr. Peterson tells May's mamma that she is looking nice, and Pappa does not appreciate it.
9. May wants to go to Smith Island to visit Amy's grave.
10. Pappa is very happy to see that May is safe, and he does not get angry at her this time.

Page 31

Accept all logical foods/beverages.

Page 43

Matching

1. Mamma
2. Grandmother Patience
3. Wilbert
4. May
5. Pappa

True or False

1. False
2. False
3. True
4. True
5. False

Short Answer

1. May feels this way because her father is always getting angry with her for getting into mischief, which he believes is not feminine.
2. Kaarlo is May's cousin. His family had to leave him with the Jacksons because they could not afford to travel with him.
3. Grandmother Patience has no patience; she is a mean woman.
4. May and Wilbert stay with Aunt Feenie because it is understood that absence from things that remind May of Baby Amy will help her grieve. Wilbert stays because May needs him for comfort.
5. Lonny has just lost his mother, and his father is a drunk. Lonny has been in his house all alone since his mother died. (Other answers may also be acceptable for these questions.)

Essay

1. Reference should be made to May leaving home periodically throughout the book, then returning stronger and wiser after each incident (retreat to Baby Island, mission to find Micah Anderson, visit to Smith Island, and her stay in Astoria).
2. Answers will vary. Accept all reasonable and well-supported responses and explanations.

Page 44

Grade students on their comprehension of the story as evidenced by the length of answers and depth of responses.

Page 45

Perform all conversations in class. Ask students to respond to the conversations by answering questions such as: "Are the conversations realistic?" or, "Are the words the characters say in keeping with their personalities?"